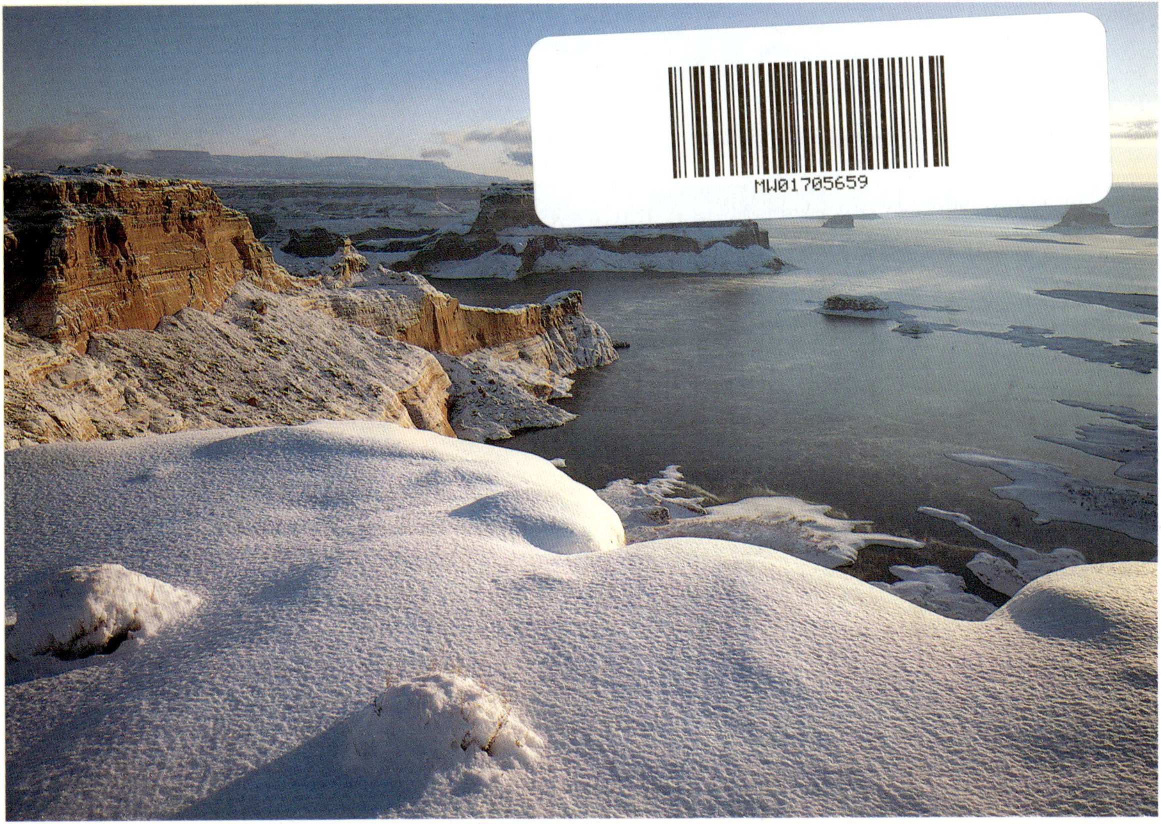

Padre Bay, Winter. Seen here from atop Romana Mesa, the enormity of Lake Powell is obvious. More than 250 square miles of deep blue water provide a spectacular contrast with the surrounding red rock landscape. At an elevation of 3,700 feet, winter snow flurries are not uncommon on the heights surrounding the lake.

FROM THE GLEN CANYON WISH YOU WERE HERE® POSTCARD BOOK

SIERRA PRESS, INC. , PO BOX 430, EL PORTAL, CA 95318

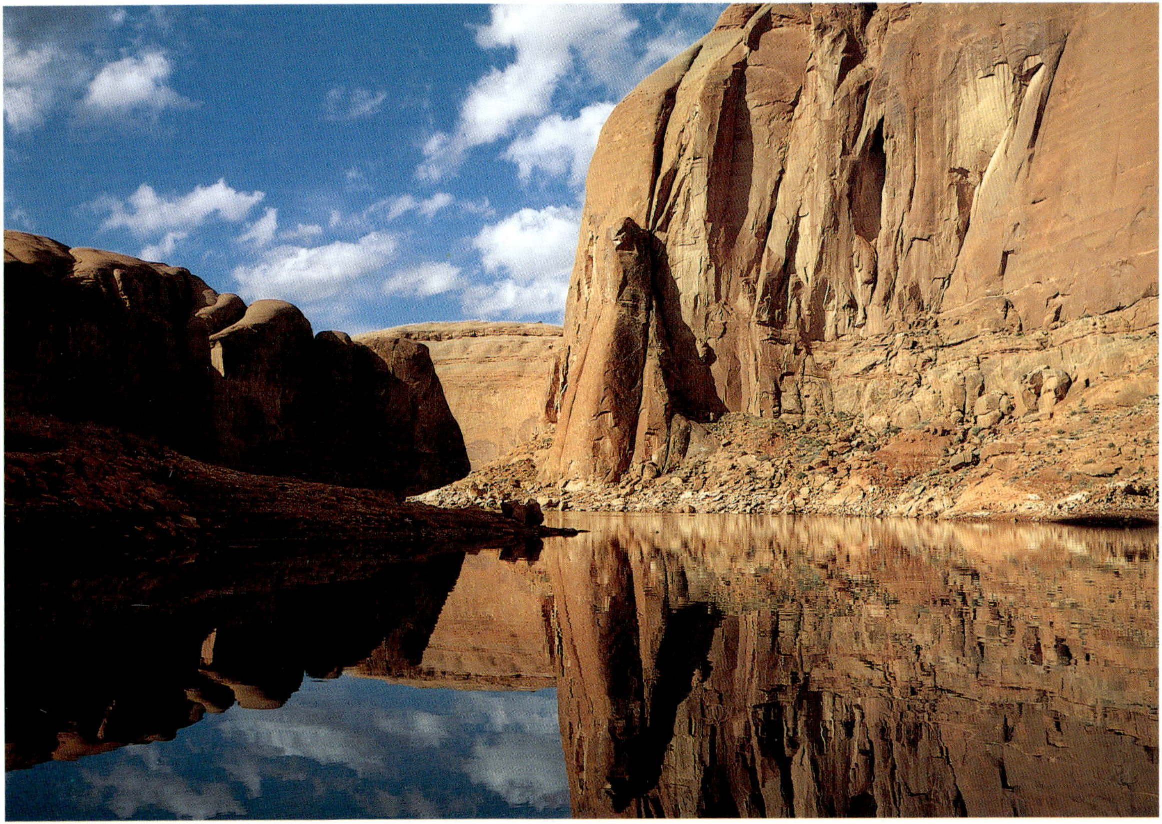

Dry Rock Creek Canyon. One of the 96 major side canyons of Lake Powell, Dry Rock Creek contains nine major coves of its own. Plunging from dizzying heights into waters which are often hundreds of feet deep, these spectacular sandstone walls are typical of many side canyons.

FROM THE GLEN CANYON WISH YOU WERE HERE® POSTCARD BOOK

SIERRA PRESS, INC., PO BOX 430, EL PORTAL, CA 95318

PHOTO: © GARY LADD

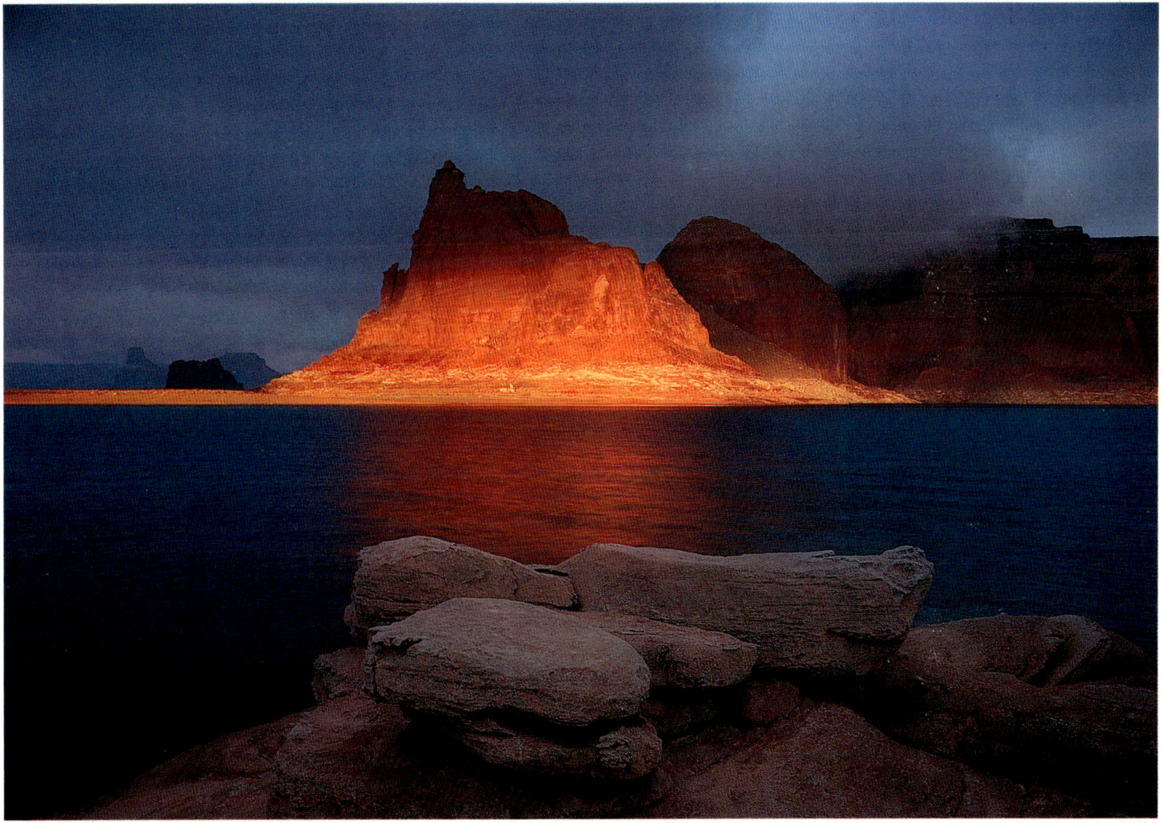

Kane Point, Sunset. Padre Butte, at the tip of Kane Point, was named in honor of Padres Dominguez and Escalante. These Franciscan explorers labored past this point in the autumn of 1776. Their hopes of establishing a route from Santa Fe to the Pacific Coast were dashed against the stony ramparts of this region.

FROM THE GLEN CANYON WISH YOU WERE HERE® POSTCARD BOOK

SIERRA PRESS, INC. , PO BOX 430, EL PORTAL, CA 95318

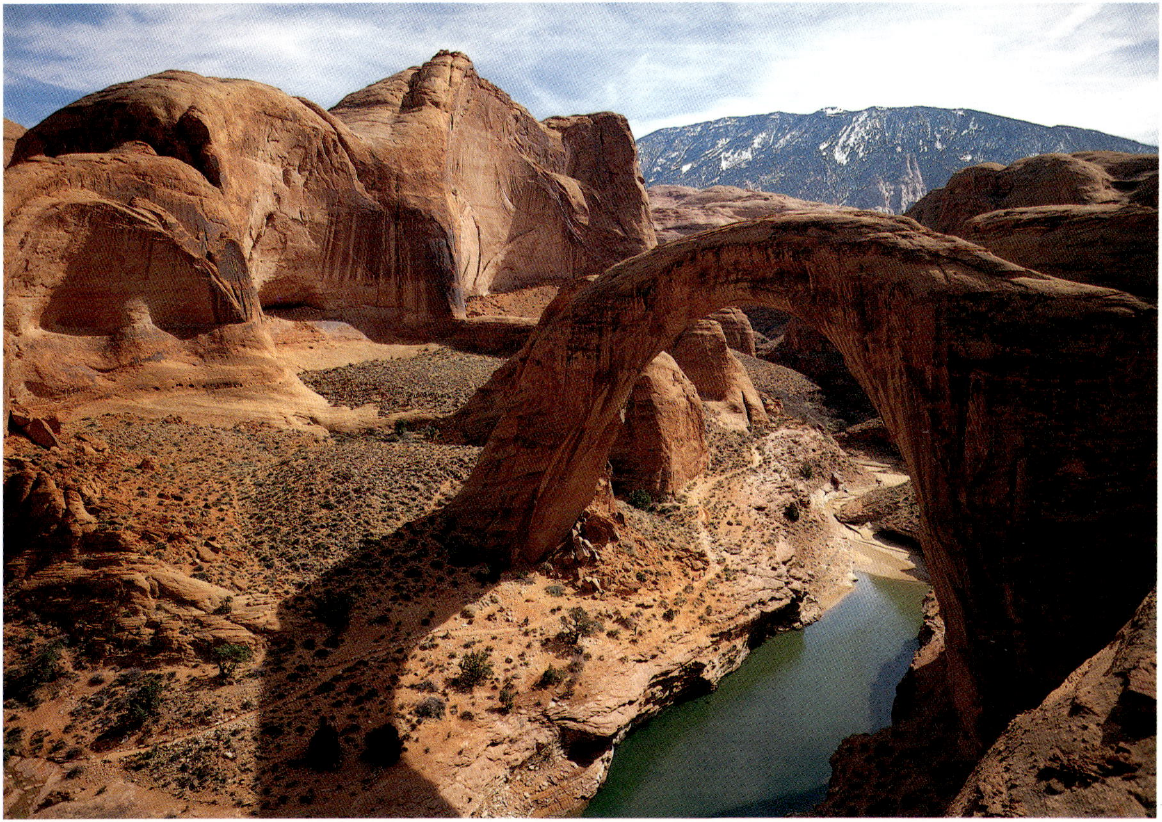

Rainbow Bridge National Monument. This breathtaking leap of stone is known to the Navajo as "Nonne-Zoshi", Rainbow of Stone. First seen by white explorers in 1909, it was established as a national monument by President Taft in 1910. Rising 290 feet above Bridge Creek it spans 275 feet and is 42 feet thick and 33 feet wide at its apex.

FROM THE GLEN CANYON WISH YOU WERE HERE® POSTCARD BOOK

SIERRA PRESS, INC. , PO BOX 430, EL PORTAL, CA 95318

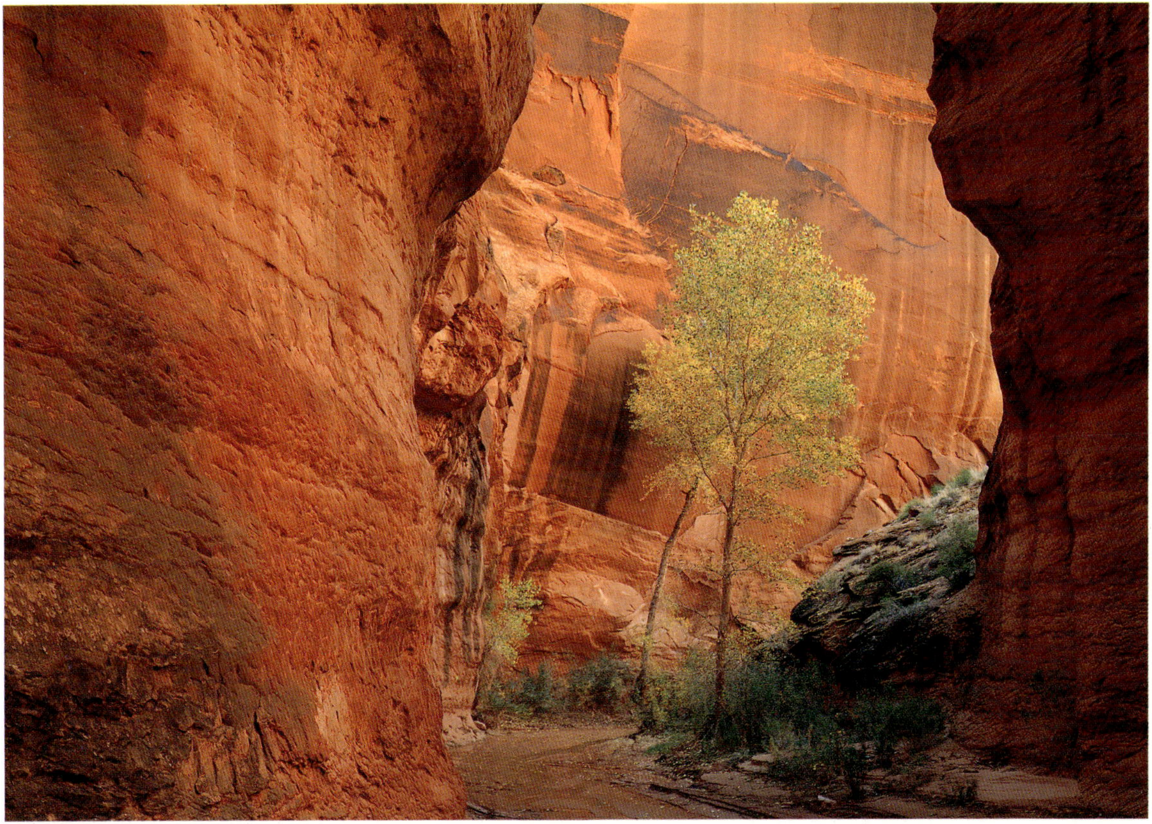

Cottonwood in unnamed Side Canyon. There are 96 major, and countless minor, side canyons surrounding Lake Powell. It is not uncommon for them to be hundreds of feet deep. Cottonwood, willow and ash; maidenhair fern, monkeyflower and columbine; beaver, coyote and canyon wren all call these canyons home.

FROM THE GLEN CANYON WISH YOU WERE HERE® POSTCARD BOOK

SIERRA PRESS, INC., PO BOX 430, EL PORTAL, CA 95318

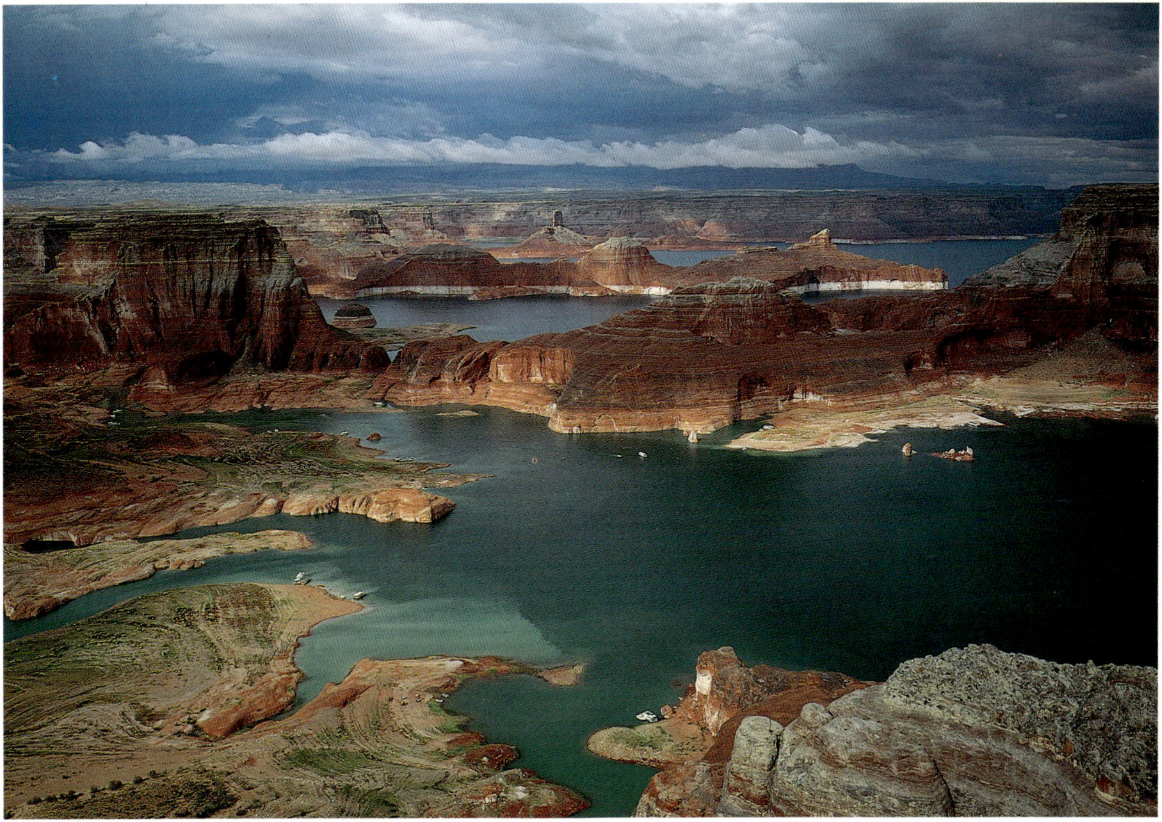

Gunsight Canyon, Padre Bay. This view of Lake Powell provides the viewer with some idea of the hardships faced by Dominguez and Escalante when they passed through this area in 1776. Their "Crossing of the Fathers", where they were finally able to ford the Colorado River, now lies beneath 500 feet of water.

FROM THE GLEN CANYON WISH YOU WERE HERE® POSTCARD BOOK

SIERRA PRESS, INC. , PO BOX 430, EL PORTAL, CA 95318

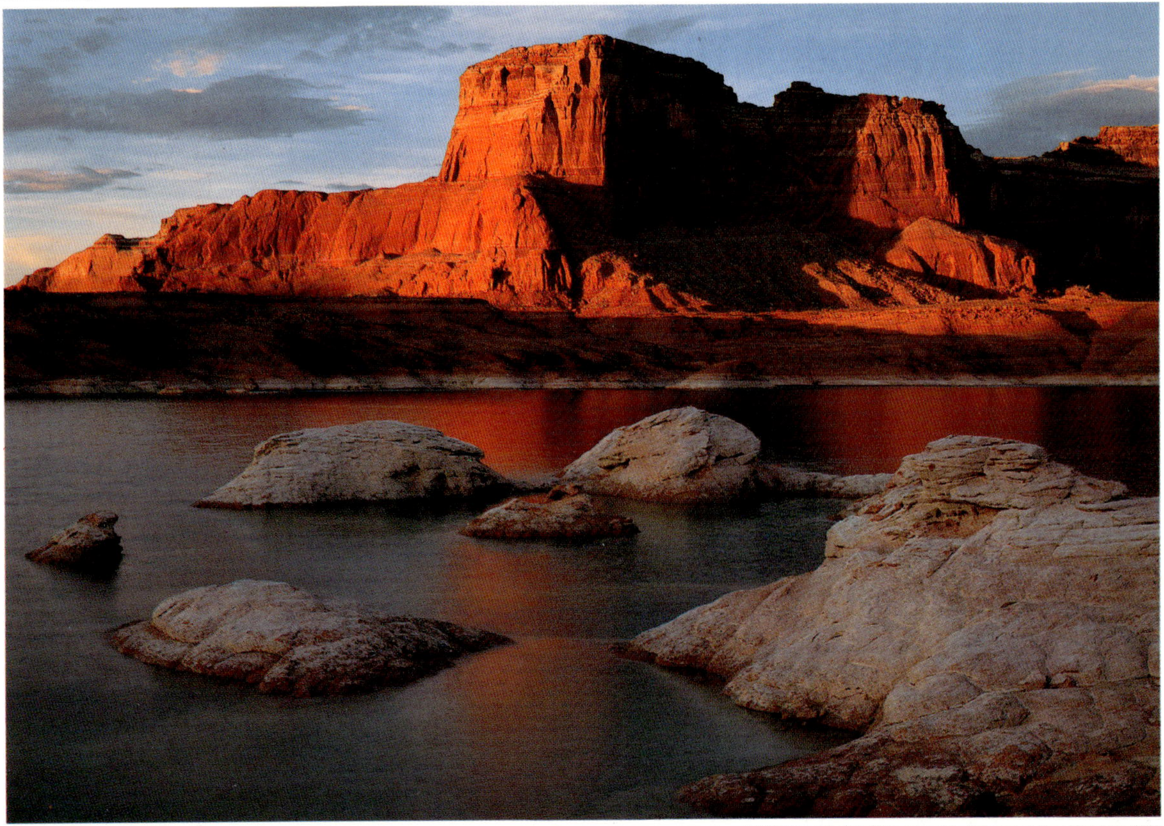

Gregory Butte, Sunset. One of the most striking features of Lake Powell is its setting. Long considered the heart of the Colorado Plateau, this region was first recommended for National Park status in 1937, when Escalante National Park was proposed. This region is home to the greatest concentration of National Parks and Monuments in the United States.

FROM THE GLEN CANYON WISH YOU WERE HERE® POSTCARD BOOK

SIERRA PRESS, INC. , PO BOX 430, EL PORTAL, CA 95318

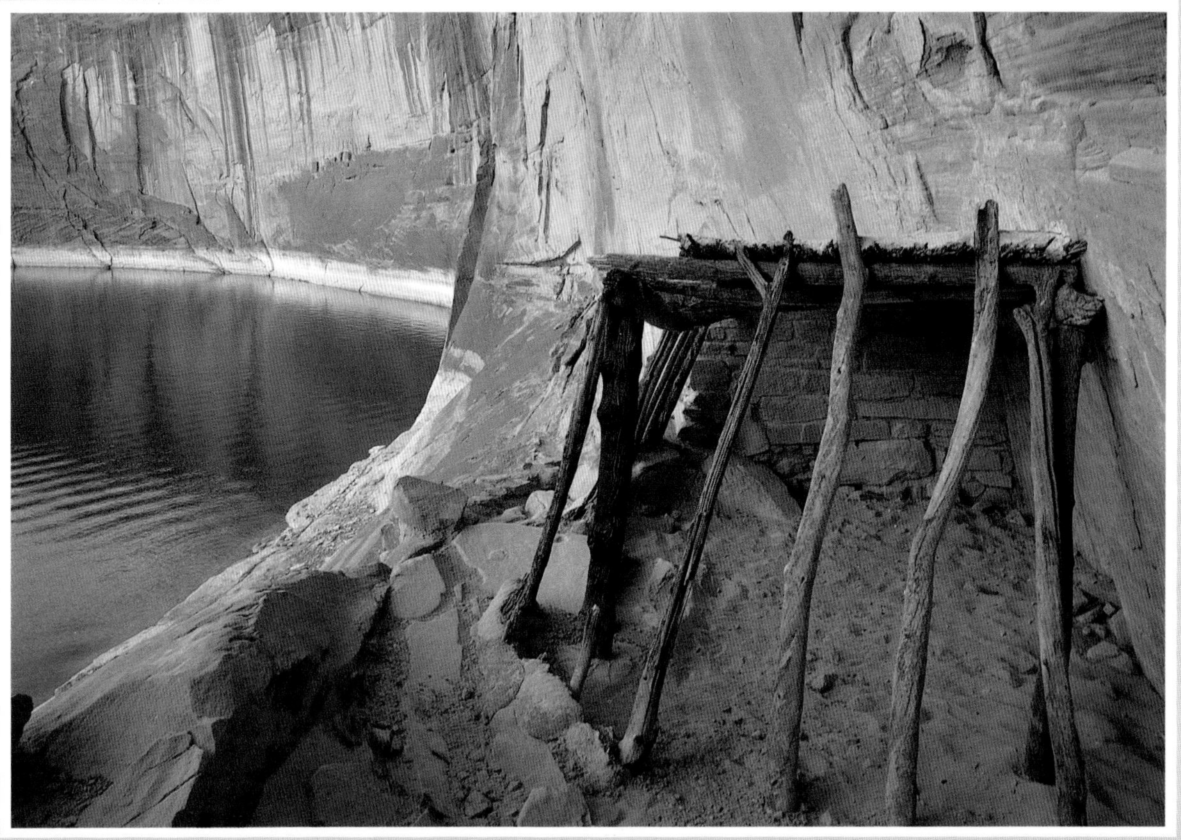

Anasazi Granary. The Colorado Plateau, despite its somewhat forbidding appearance, has supported a human population, often greater than today's, for at least thirty centuries. This small granary was used to store precious stocks of corn, squash and beans, keeping them dry and out of reach of rodents. Although many have been submerged, structures such as this are still found in many canyons around the lake.

FROM THE GLEN CANYON WISH YOU WERE HERE® POSTCARD BOOK

SIERRA PRESS, INC., PO BOX 430, EL PORTAL, CA 95318

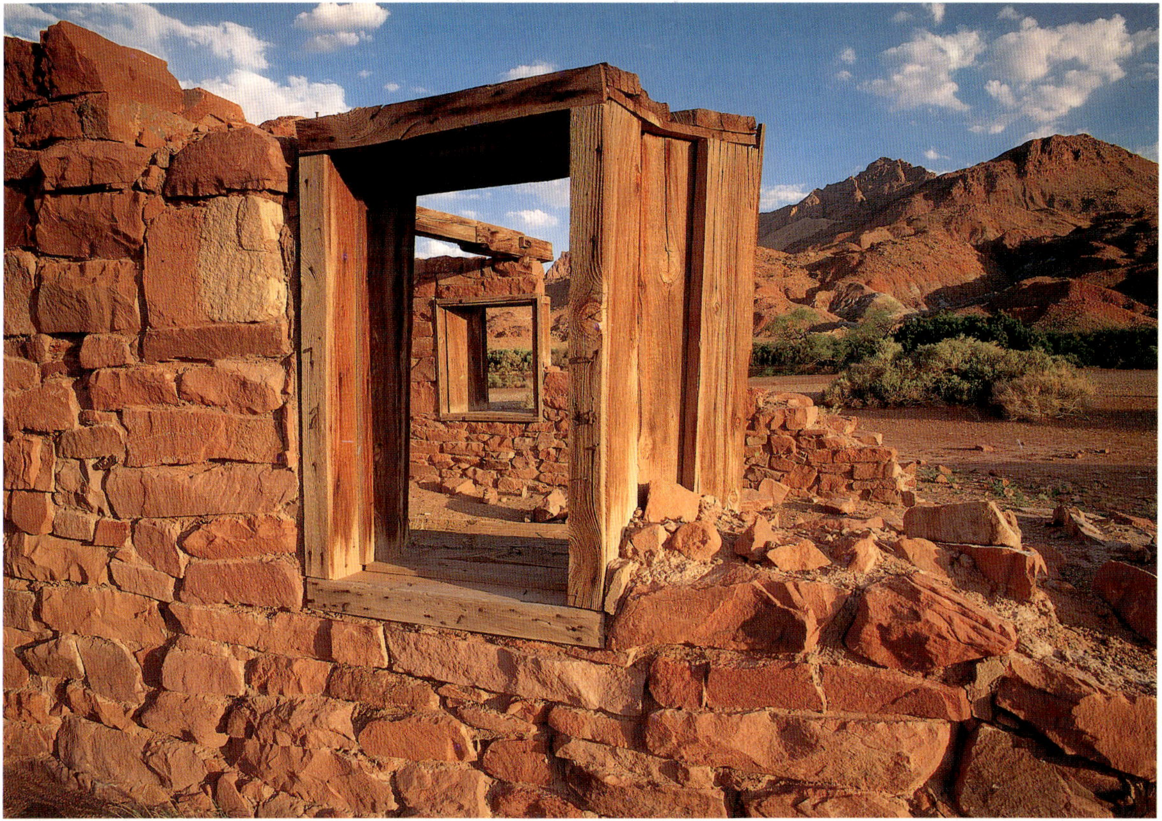

Fort at Lees Ferry. Situated near the confluence of the Paria and Colorado Rivers, the buildings at "Lonely Dell Ranch" were built by John D. Lee for his seventeenth wife, Emma, in 1872. He had been dispatched by the Mormon Church to provide a ferry service at this natural crossing located between Glen and Marble Canyons. The ferry was operated until 1928 when a bridge was finally constructed near this site.

FROM THE GLEN CANYON WISH YOU WERE HERE® POSTCARD BOOK

SIERRA PRESS, INC., PO BOX 430, EL PORTAL, CA 95318

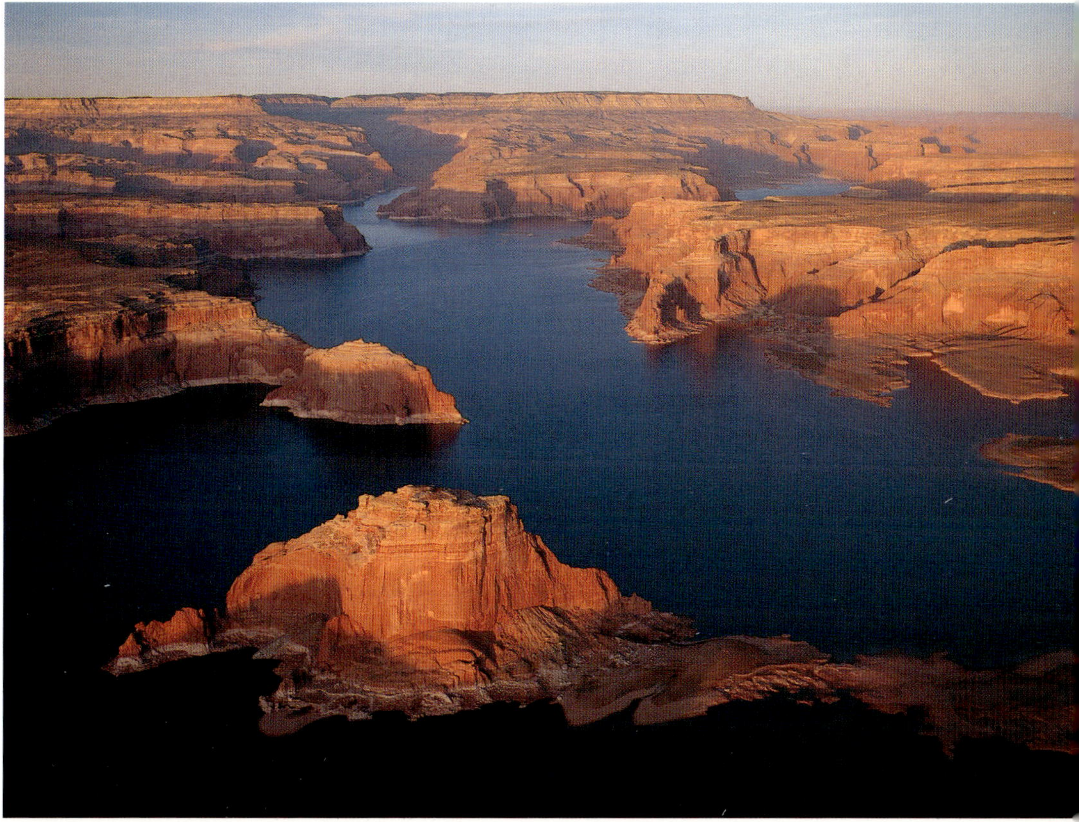

Gregory Butte and Lake Powell, Sunset. Seen here from an aerial perspective, the size of Lake Powell is obvious. One of the largest artificially created lakes on Earth, at full capacity it has 250 square miles of surface area, reaches 186 miles up the Colorado River, has nearly 2,000 miles of shoreline and is more than 500 feet deep at the dam.

FROM THE GLEN CANYON WISH YOU WERE HERE® POSTCARD BOOK

SIERRA PRESS, INC. , PO BOX 430, EL PORTAL, CA 95318

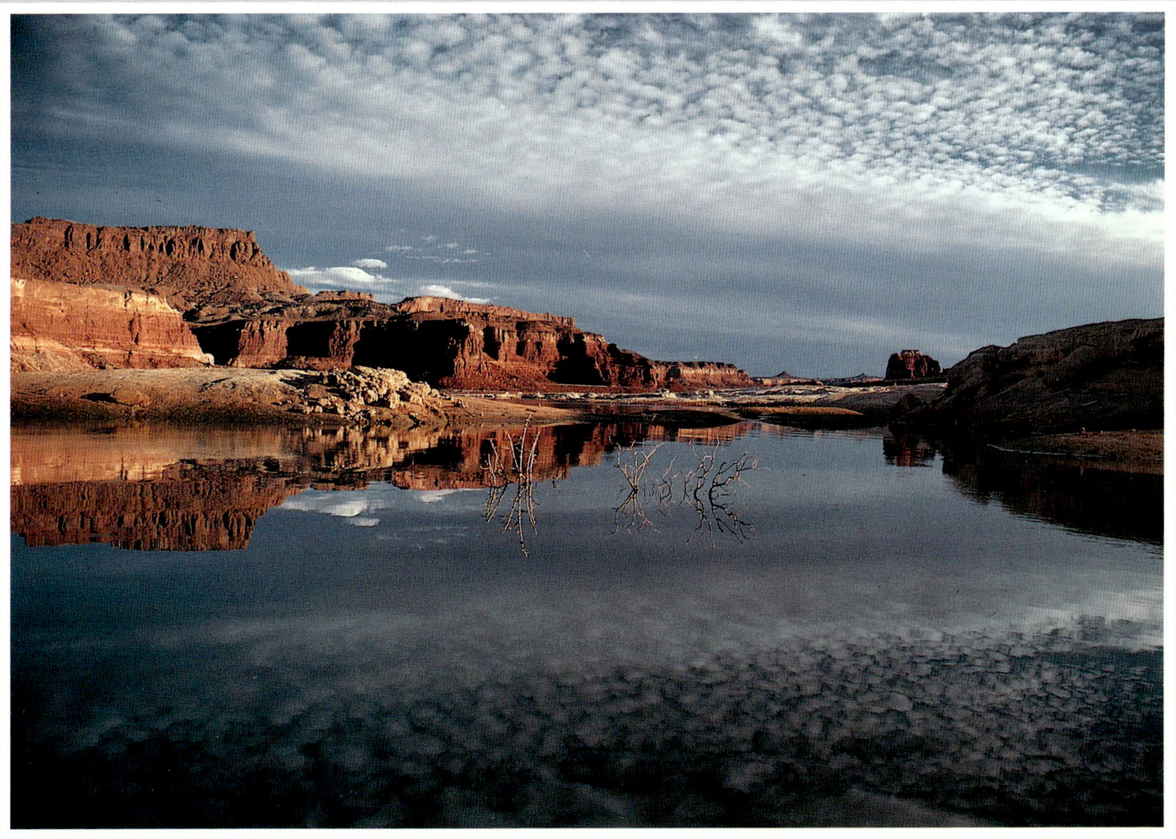

Dawn near Hite. The original site of Cass Hite's "Dandy Crossing" now lies beneath the waters of Lake Powell. Located near the confluence of the Colorado and Dirty Devil Rivers, this was a popular gathering spot for nineteenth century trappers and traders. Not only was it an easy crossing of the Colorado, but the only post office in Glen Canyon was here as well.

FROM THE GLEN CANYON WISH YOU WERE HERE® POSTCARD BOOK

SIERRA PRESS, INC. , PO BOX 430, EL PORTAL, CA 95318

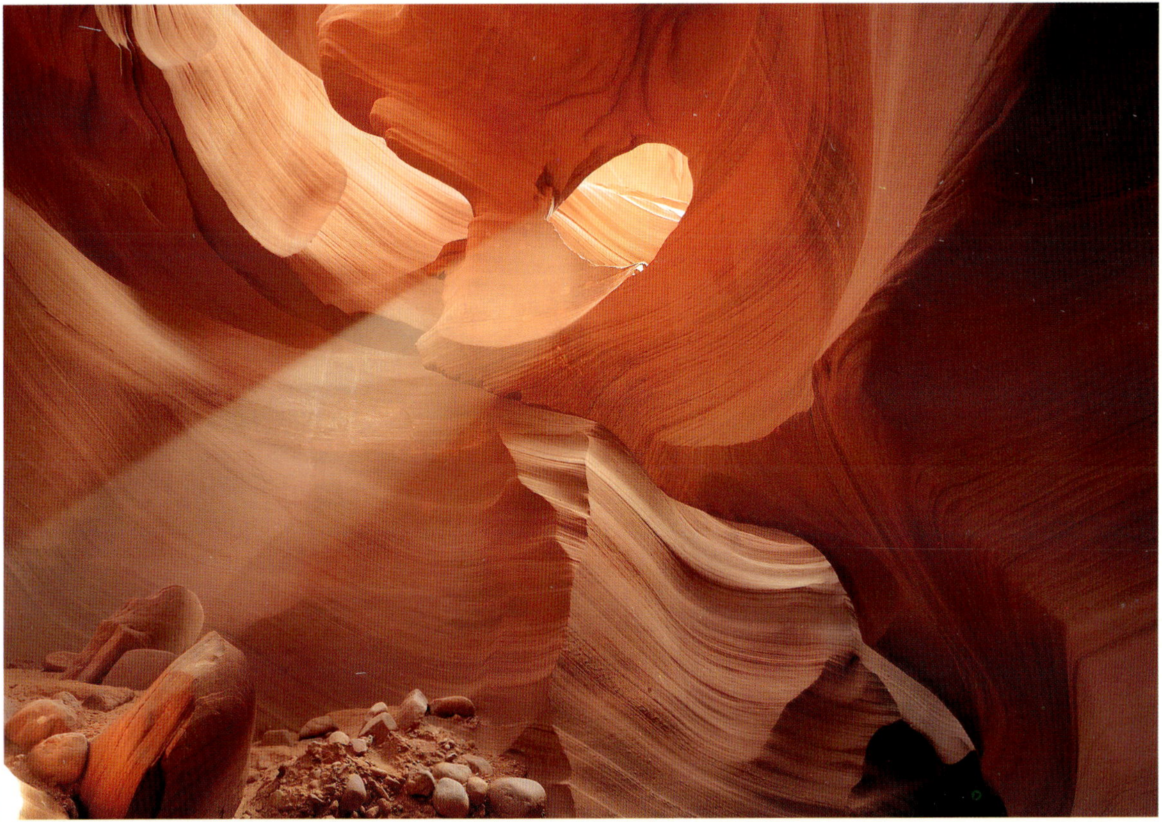

Lower Antelope Canyon. Water and time have eroded the Navajo sandstone found in this region into remarkable forms of complex beauty, none more astonishing than "slot canyons". These narrow defiles, often no more than a few feet wide, are deeply etched into the landscape and often go unseen. A permit is required to visit many slots as they are on Navajo land.

SIERRA PRESS, INC. , PO BOX 430, EL PORTAL, CA 95318

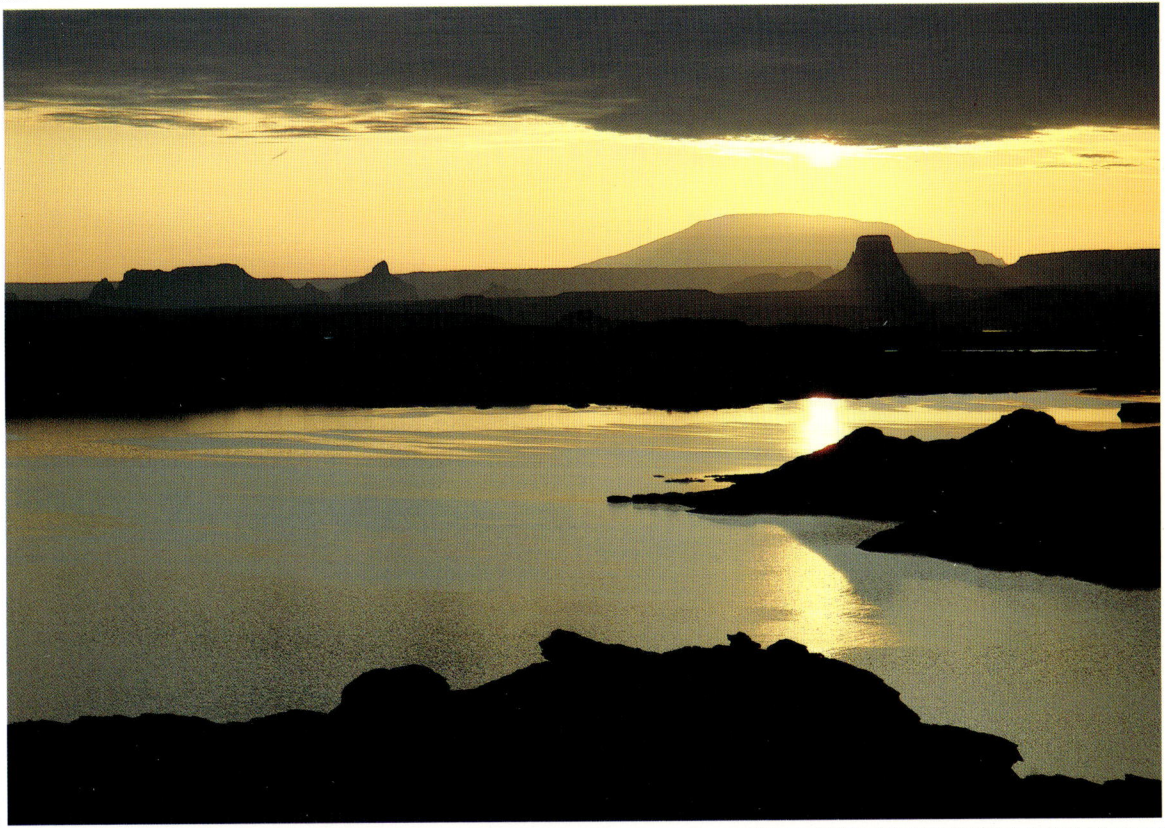

Navajo Mountain, Sunrise. The mammoth hulk of Navajo Mountain, which rises nearly 7,000 feet above lake level, is visible from many points around the Colorado Plateau. Its 48 million-year-old igneous flanks have been eroded into a tortured landscape of convoluted canyons. Water flowing from its heights was responsible for the formation of Rainbow Bridge.

FROM THE GLEN CANYON WISH YOU WERE HERE® POSTCARD BOOK

SIERRA PRESS, INC. , PO BOX 430, EL PORTAL, CA 95318

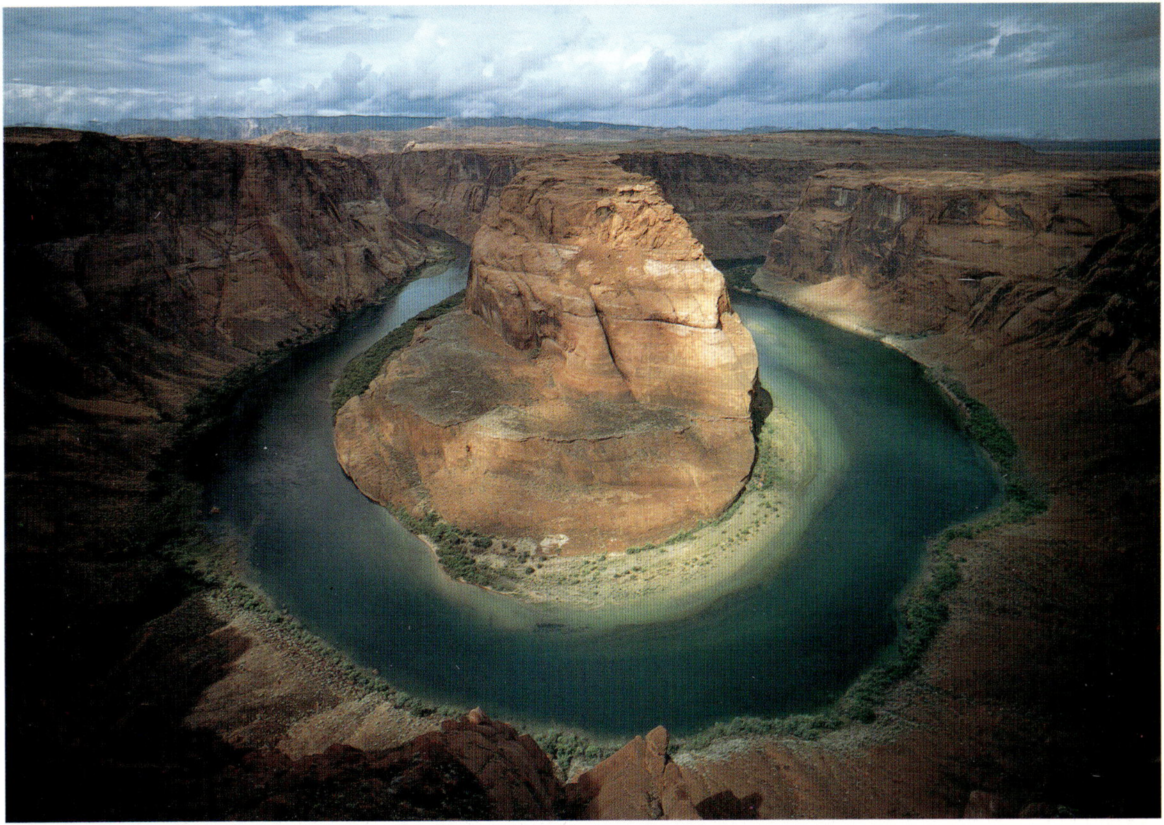

Horseshoe Bend, Colorado River. The 15 miles of the Colorado River between Glen Canyon Dam and Lees Ferry are very different today than when John Wesley Powell first explored the region in 1868. The cold, clear water released at the dam today is a far cry from the warm, muddy waters which gave the river its name originally.

FROM THE GLEN CANYON WISH YOU WERE HERE® POSTCARD BOOK

SIERRA PRESS, INC. , PO BOX 430, EL PORTAL, CA 95318